Please return/renew this item
by the last date shown.
Books may also be renewed by
phone and Internet.

THE
REVISION
SERIES

www.How2Become.com

As part of this product you have also received FREE access to online tests that will help you to pass Key Stage 2 SCIENCE *(Chemistry)*.

To gain access, simply go to:

www.PsychometricTestsOnline.co.uk

Get more products
for passing any test at:

www.How2Become.com

Orders: Please contact How2Become Ltd, Suite 14, 50 Churchill Square Business Centre, Kings Hill, Kent ME19 4YU.

You can order through Amazon.co.uk under ISBN 9781910602911, via the website www.How2Become.com or through Gardners.com.

ISBN: 9781910602911

First published in 2016 by How2Become Ltd.

Typeset for How2Become Ltd by Anton Pshinka.

Disclaimer

Every effort has been made to ensure that the information contained within this guide is accurate at the time of publication. How2Become Ltd is not responsible for anyone failing any part of any selection process as a result of the information contained within this guide. How2Become Ltd and their authors cannot accept any responsibility for any errors or omissions within this guide, however caused. No responsibility for loss or damage occasioned by any person acting, or refraining from action, as a result of the material in this publication can be accepted by How2Become Ltd.

The information within this guide does not represent the views of any third party service or organisation.

CONTENTS

THE
REVISION
SERIES

GUIDANCE FOR PARENTS

Whilst the SATs are a daunting, disliked and often maligned concept, they remain an essential part of a child's education. Children should be provided with the best tools and guidance to enhance their intellectual ability and improve their performance.

The purpose of this section is to guide you through the KS2 Science (Chemistry) exam. It will allow you to familiarise yourself with all of the important information, advice and tips that your child will need in order to achieve exam success.

The NEW SATs

From the summer of 2016, the SATs will undergo considerable changes, as dictated by the new national curriculum.

The purpose of the new and revised SATs is to ensure these tests remain rigorous, and therefore prove to be of a much higher standard compared to previous years.

With the new national curriculum comes a new marking scheme. Whilst we cannot provide details of exactly what this marking scheme consists of, we know that your child's tests will be marked externally. The scores of these tests will be used to monitor the progress of each school's performance, which is done via Ofsted reports and League tables.

Ultimately, your child's scores in their SATs will be used in conjunction with classroom assessments, to provide a general overview of their attainment and progression during that academic year.

For more information on the new national curriculum, please visit the Department for Education section of the Government's website.

When Do the New SATs Come into Place?

The new national curriculum for Key Stage 2 SATs will be assessed for the first time in May 2016.

What do the New SATs Cover?

The national curriculum for Key Stage 2 SATs will consist of the following:

- English Reading (Comprehension)
- English Grammar (Grammar, Punctuation and Spelling)
- Maths (Arithmetic and Reasoning)
- Science (Biology, Chemistry, Physics)*

*(*Please note that not all children completing the SATs will sit a Science SAT. A selection of schools will be required to take part in a science sampling every other year.)*

For more revision guides including KS2 Biology and Physics, as well as KS2 Science Practice Papers, please visit www.amazon.co.uk, and type the book title into Search:

Top Tips For Parents

In order for your child to score highly in their SATs, you need to ensure that they have everything they need to achieve high marks!

It is important that you and your child are fully aware of what the SATs consist of. The more familiar you are with what to expect, the better their chances will be when they sit down to take the tests.

Below is a list of GOLDEN NUGGETS that will help you AND your child to prepare for the Key Stage 2 SATs.

- ## Golden Nugget 1 – Revision timetables

When it comes to exams, preparation is key. That is why you need to sit down with your child and come up with an efficient and well-structured revision timetable.

It is important that you work with your child to assess their academic strengths and weaknesses, in order to carry out these revision sessions successfully.

TIP – Focus on their weaker areas first!

TIP – Create a weekly revision timetable to work through different subject areas.

TIP – Spend time revising with your child. Your child will benefit from your help and this is a great way for you to monitor their progress.

- ## Golden Nugget 2 – Understanding the best way your child learns

There are many different ways to revise when it comes to exams, and it all comes down to picking a way that your child will find most useful.

Below is a list of the common learning styles that you may want to try with your child:

- **Visual** – the use of pictures and images to remember information.

- **Aural** – the use of sound and music to remember information.

- **Verbal** – the use of words, in both speech and writing, to understand information.

- **Social** – working together in groups.

- **Solitary** – working and studying alone.

Popular revision techniques include: *mind mapping; flash cards; making notes; drawing flow charts* and *diagrams.* You could instruct your child on how to turn diagrams and pictures into words, and words into diagrams. Try as many different methods as possible to see which is the most successful for your child's learning.

> *TIP* – *Work out what kind of learner your child is. What method will they benefit from the most?*
>
> *TIP* – *Try a couple of different learning aids and see if you notice a change in your child's ability to understand what is being taught.*

• Golden Nugget 3 – Break times

Allow your child plenty of breaks when revising.

It's really important not to overwork your child, particularly for tests such as the SATs which are not marked on a pass or fail basis.

> *TIP* – *Practising for 10 to 15 minutes per day will improve your child's understanding of the topic being revised.*

• Golden Nugget 4 – Practice, practice and more practice!

Purchase past practice papers. Although the curriculum will have changed for 2016, practice papers are still a fantastic way for you to gain an idea of how your child is likely to be tested.

- ## Golden Nugget 5 – Variety is key!

Make sure that your child reads a variety of chemistry modules. This will be required if they wish to score high marks overall on their Science exam.

> *TIP – Spend some time with your child writing a list of all the key areas and topics that need to be covered. This way, your child will be able to tailor their revision to each module.*

- ## Golden Nugget 6 – Encourage your child to discuss their work

When your child is undergoing practice questions, ask your child to talk about what they have just read. Did they understand it? Did they know what all the words meant?

> *TIP – Sit down with your child and ask them questions about what they have just learnt. Have them discuss the work with you. Have they understood everything? Are there any grey areas that they are unsure of?*

- ## Golden Nugget 7 – Stay positive!

The most important piece of preparation advice we can give you is to make sure that your child is positive and relaxed about these tests.

Don't let the SATs worry you, and certainly don't let them worry your child.

> *TIP – Make sure the home environment is as comfortable and relaxed as possible for your child.*

- ## Golden Nugget 8 – Answer the easier questions first

A good tip to teach your child is to answer all the questions they find easiest first. That way, they can swiftly work through the questions before attempting the questions they struggle with.

TIP – Get your child to undergo a practice paper. Tell them to fill in the answers that they find the easiest first. That way, you can spend time helping your child with the questions they find more difficult.

Spend some time working through the questions they find difficult and make sure that they know how to work out the answer.

THE REVISION SERIES

ROCKS AND FOSSILS

ROCKS AND FOSSILS

Rocks and Fossils

In this first chapter, we are going to be looking at all things to do with rocks. You might not think there is a great deal that you can say about a rock, but in actual fact, there's loads of interesting things to know about rocks!

Rocks have existed almost as long as the Earth has, and play a vital role in the Earth's formation.

We humans have used all kinds of rocks for as long as we have been on Earth, and we would not have been able to survive without them.

Our superhero Freddie is going to teach you **FOUR** main things about rocks!

1. **What is a rock?**

2. **Different types of rock**

3. **Soil**

4. **Fossils**

So let's get into it, starting with section 1!

ROCKS AND FOSSILS

What is a rock?

'Rock' is how we describe the masses of minerals (and other material) that have formed together over millions of years to make up what we see all around us. Rocks can be **hard, soft** and everything **in-between**.

Also, rocks can come in almost any size imaginable – from pebbles to boulders. 'Rock' is even how we refer to the sections of the Earth that are not made up of water!

'Rock' is a very broad term that can be used to describe many different kinds of material. Rocks can be hard, soft, permeable and impermeable.

See the next page for more!

ROCKS AND FOSSILS

Types of rocks

HARD ROCKS

Hard rocks are difficult to break apart. Heavy tools are needed to do so.

These rocks can be polished to become smooth and shiny – the act of polishing does not damage them.

These rocks are very useful for humans. In the past, many of our tools and buildings were made out of hard rocks, because they can withstand strong force/weather conditions.

Granite and marble

SOFT ROCKS

Soft rocks are easier to break apart. They often crumble without too much effort.

These rocks can also be very useful to humans, as they can be manipulated easily. For example, chalk (made from limestone) has been used by humans for centuries for writing: it is soft enough to crumble and leave a mark on other objects.

Chalk

ROCKS AND FOSSILS

PERMEABLE ROCKS

If a rock is 'permeable', then water is able to soak into it. Some permeable rocks can hold water, and others can let water pass all the way through them. Most permeable rocks are also 'soft rocks'.

Permeable rocks can also be called 'porous' rocks.

Limestone and sandstone

IMPERMEABLE ROCKS

An impermeable rock does not allow water to soak into it; water will just run off it. Most impermeable rocks are also 'hard rocks' – the fact that they are impermeable helps with many of their main uses (e.g. slate rooves).

Impermeable rocks can also be called 'non-porous' rocks.

Slate

ROCKS AND FOSSILS

Soil

Soil, which covers huge areas of Earth's land, naturally forms over millions of years, and has four main ingredients.

Rock is a vital ingredient in nearly all types of soil. Soil consists of tiny pieces comprising **rock, dead plants and animals, water** and **air**. Soil also contains a variety of living things like bacteria and other microorganisms.

Soil is vital for life on Earth because it provides an ideal place for plants to grow. Soil contains the water and nutrients that they need, and does not restrict the plant's growth.

Soil can be sandy, silty, or clay:

SANDY: Soil with the largest particles of rock. Sandy soil is dry and gritty, and cannot hold on to water because the large particles are too far apart.

SILTY: Soil which has much smaller particles of rock than sandy soil, so it is much better at holding water. Silty soil can be compacted much more easily.

CLAY: Soil which contains the smallest particles of rock, so it is very good at holding water. This also means that it can hold more nutrients in a smaller space, so clay soil is ideal for nurturing plants.

Sandy soil, silty soil and clay soil

ROCKS AND FOSSILS

Fossils

WHAT IS A FOSSIL?

Fossils are the remains of plants or animals that lived on Earth millions of years ago, preserved until today through sheer chance. *(See the next page for more on how fossils are formed!)*

Fossils need to have perfect conditions in order to form. Most dinosaur remains simply waste away into the ground.

The fact that fossils take millions of years to form shows us that all fossils discovered by humans are of animals which are long-extinct or ancestors of modern animals.

WHAT DO FOSSILS SHOW US?

Fossils prove the existence of dinosaurs and other extinct species. Without them, we would not know that dinosaurs existed.

They can also tell us how long ago these animals existed, and where they lived. They also tell us about their diet and behaviour.

Some of the best-preserved and most complete fossils can show us near-perfect images of the skeletons of dinosaurs and other ancient animals.

ROCKS AND FOSSILS

HOW ARE FOSSILS FORMED?

1. An animal **dies**, and its **remains sink to the sea bed** (a land animal's remains are swept into the ocean where they sink).

2. The **animal's skin, flesh, and organs rot away,** leaving the skeleton. The **skeleton is eventually buried by mud or sand** (sediment).

3. **The skeleton gets buried deeper** and deeper as more and more sediment is added by the swirling water. This means that the skeleton is put under **more and more pressure** by the increasing number of layers of mud it is squashed by.

4. Eventually, the skeleton is buried extremely deeply below the sea floor. By this point, there is **so much force** (from the pressure) **acting on the sediment** surrounding the bones, that **it turns into rock.**

ROCKS AND FOSSILS

5. As more time passes, the **bones slowly get dissolved** as they sit in ground water. This leaves a **mould** (inside the rock) of the exact shape of the skeleton.

6. Water then pours in and out of the mould and fills the space left by the bones. While the water flows in and out, it deposits minerals into the mould. Eventually, these **minerals completely fill the space, making a solid cast.**

7. Finally, over millions of years, the cast (encased with rock) **begins to rise** to the surface of the Earth. Once there, the rock is **gradually worn away, revealing the fossil.**

Question 1

Anil and Lalita need your help! They need to decide which of the rocks in the list below are most suited to each situation they are looking at. Look at the list, and write 'Marble', 'Chalk', 'Slate' or 'Granite' next to the most suitable situation in the space provided.

> ### List of Rocks
>
> • *Marble – attractive in appearance but hard-wearing and impermeable. Can be carved and polished to a great sheen.*
>
> • *Chalk – Can be stained different colours and is soft enough to wear away very easily, leaving a mark on most surfaces.*
>
> • *Slate – hard and impermeable, but not too dense. Can be cut into thin but strong sheets.*
>
> • *Granite – Very hard, dense and impermeable rock that is very difficult to wear down.*

1. Drawing a colourful mural on the black playground floor.

    ☐

2. Building the steps and outside walls of a great castle.

    ☐

3. Creating an elaborate but sturdy monument – like a statue or a fountain.

    ☐

4. Crafting many roof tiles to keep your house dry.

    ☐

Question 2

Look at the following diagrams of different types of soil. Read their descriptions and decide whether the soil is 'Sandy, 'Silty' and 'Clay'.

Made up of very small particles of rock, and is able to be compacted with ease:

_____

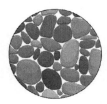

Made up of larger particles of rock. Poor at holding onto water, so can often be too dry to sustain plant life:

_____

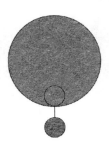

Made up of extremely small particles of rock. Very good at holding water but can become too hard in a short space of time:

_____

Question 3

Scarlett has made a list of facts about fossils. Unfortunately, Blaze has got his hands on it and has snuck some in that just aren't true! Defeat Blaze and help Scarlett by deciding who wrote each statement. Circle Scarlett for the TRUE statements and circle Blaze for the FALSE statements.

1. **Fossils are very rare – conditions have to be perfect for a fossil to form.**

SCARLETT   BLAZE

2. **Humans have discovered fossils of modern animals as we see them today.**

SCARLETT   BLAZE

3. **Fossils prove the existence of dinosaurs.**

SCARLETT   BLAZE

4. Fossils can give us an insight into the diet and behaviour of dinosaurs.

SCARLETT

BLAZE

5. Humans have discovered every fossil in the world.

SCARLETT

BLAZE

Question 4

Below are the steps that an animal skeleton goes through during the process of fossilisation. However, they are in the wrong order! Rearrange them correctly in the spaces below:

The sediment around the skeleton turns to rock

An animal dies and sinks to the bottom of the ocean

The skeleton starts to get buried by more and more sediment

The rock around the cast rises to the surface and wears away, exposing the fossil

The skeleton is dissolved by ground water, leaving a mould in the rock

Water fills the mould, and minerals eventually form a solid cast

The animal's soft parts rot away, leaving only its skeleton

1. _____

2. _____

3. _____

4. _____

5. _____

6. _____

7. _____

ANSWERS TO ROCKS AND SOIL

Question 1

1. Chalk
2. Granite
3. Marble
4. Slate

Question 2

Made up of very small particles of rock, and is able to be compacted with ease:

Silty soil

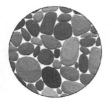

Made up of larger particles of rock. Poor at holding onto water, so can often be too dry to sustain plant life:

Sandy soil

Made up of extremely small particles of rock. Very good at holding water but can become too hard in a short space of time:

Clay soil

Question 3

1. SCARLETT
2. BLAZE
3. SCARLETT
4. SCARLETT
5. BLAZE

Question 4

1. An animal dies and sinks to the bottom of the ocean
2. The animal's soft parts rot away, leaving only its skeleton
3. The skeleton starts to gets buried by more and more sediment
4. The sediment around the skeleton turns to rock
5. The skeleton is dissolved by ground water, leaving a mould in the rock
6. Water fills the mould, and minerals eventually form a solid cast
7. The rock around the cast rises to the surface and wears away, exposing the fossil

STATES
OF MATTER

STATES OF MATTER

STATES OF MATTER

In this chapter, we will look at what makes a material a solid, a liquid, or a gas, and what causes certain materials to change from one state to another.

This will include looking at the water cycle, and the physical processes involved such as evaporation and condensation.

Our superhero Anil is going to show you **THREE** main things about states!

1. **Solids, liquids, and gases**

2. **Changing states**

3. **The water cycle**

So let's get into it, starting with solids, liquids, and gases!

STATES OF MATTER

Solids, liquids & gases

The vast majority of materials ('things') on Earth exist as solids, liquids, or gases. These three states of matter all have very different properties and behave in different ways under different conditions.

First, let's look at what makes a solid a solid, a liquid a liquid, and a gas a gas:

SOLIDS

Solids have the firmest shape of the three states of matter; they do not flow like liquids or spread themselves out like gases.

Solids can be physically held, and stay the same shape unless acted on by an outside force. Similarly, solids stay in one place unless moved by an outside force.

SOLIDS - Like the food we eat.

STATES OF MATTER

LIQUIDS

Liquids have a much looser shape than solids; they can be poured easily and cannot be physically held without a container.

Liquids move to fill the shape of the container they are in. If they are not held by a container, they will move as far as gravity will take them.

LIQUIDS - Like the water we drink.

GASES

Gases have the loosest shape of all the three states of matter, so they are the hardest to contain. Similarly to liquids, gases spread themselves out to fill whatever space they are in. Whilst gases are affected by gravity, they are not affected in the same ways as liquids or solids.

Gases are often invisible.

GASES - Like the air we breathe.

STATES OF MATTER

Changing
states

It is possible for things to change between the states of matter. For example, there are things you can do to certain solids that will change them into a liquid, and vice-versa. Let's look at how all states can change, and what makes them do it.

SOLIDS TO LIQUIDS

Adding enough heat to most solids will turn them into a liquid. This is called **melting**.

For example:

- Taking an ice cube out of the freezer and leaving it on a table will cause it to melt and become water – room temperature is warm enough to melt ice.

- Putting a bar of gold into a furnace will cause it to melt and become liquid gold – extreme heat is needed to melt gold.

STATES OF MATTER

LIQUIDS TO SOLIDS

Cooling a liquid (making it cold) can turn it into a solid. This is called **freezing**.

For example:

- Putting a tray of water into a kitchen freezer will create ice cubes. Water freezes at zero degrees Celsius (0°C).

- Putting a container of mercury (the liquid used in thermometers) into an industrial freezer will cause it to freeze. Mercury freezes at minus 38 degrees Celsius (-38°C).

LIQUIDS TO GASES

Adding enough heat to a liquid can turn it into a gas. This is called **boiling**.

For example:

- Putting a pot of water on the hob will generate steam, as the water boils and becomes a gas.

- A puddle that forms during a rainstorm will turn into water vapour (a gas) when it is sunny. The heat of the sun causes the rainfall to be dried up and turn into water vapour – This is called evaporation.

STATES OF MATTER

GASES TO LIQUIDS

Cooling a gas can make it turn into a liquid. This is called **condensation**.

For example:

- Warm air that is heavy with water vapour comes into contact with a cold pane of glass (a window). This causes the gas to turn into liquid water, which begins to drip down the window.

- Warm air in the kitchen comes into contact with a cold jug of milk on the table. The coldness causes the air to condense on the side of the jug, and form as water.

A SUMMARY!

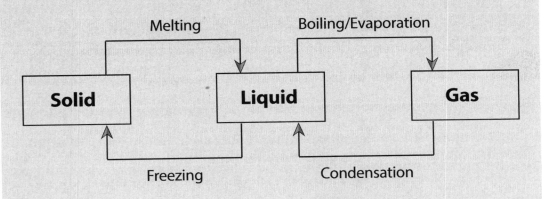

Melting   Boiling/Evaporation

Solid   **Liquid**   **Gas**

Freezing   Condensation

STATES OF MATTER

The water cycle is the constant process that water goes through on Earth. All water on Earth is constantly recycled, and goes through many different states when it does so: seawater to vapour, vapour to rainwater, rainwater to seawater.

Look at the diagram below and follow the journey that water makes, to and from the sea!

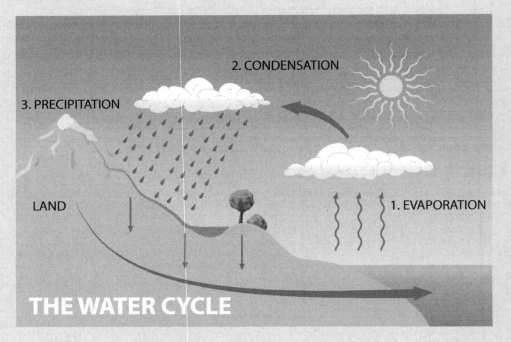

2. CONDENSATION

3. PRECIPITATION

LAND

1. EVAPORATION

THE WATER CYCLE

1. Evaporation

The sun's heat turns as much water as it can into water vapour. Most of this vapour comes from large rivers and seas.

This newly-created water vapour is a gas, so it rises from the surface of the earth, high into the air.

2. Condensation

The water vapour eventually reaches air that is so cold that condensation occurs; it turns into tiny droplets of water that are able to cluster together.

Eventually, enough water vapour has turned into water droplets that whole clouds begin to form.

3. Precipitation

When the clouds become too heavy, and enough water vapour has condensed, water begins to fall to Earth as rain, snow, or sleet.

Water that falls as precipitation into lakes and rivers will eventually be carried back to the sea.

Question 1

Match the properties of the three states of matter to the boxes reading 'Solid', 'Liquid' or 'Gas' by drawing lines.

Some properties are correct for more than one state of matter, so some boxes may need two lines drawn out of them. The first one has been done as an example.

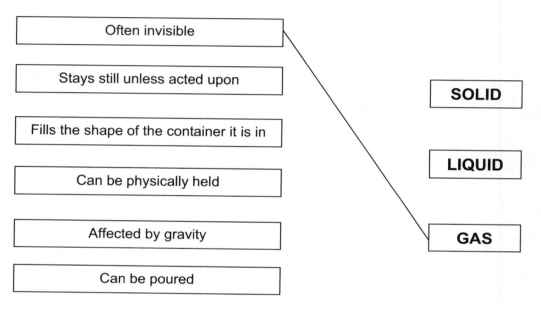

Question 2

Below are three words that describe the processes that solids, liquids and gases go through when changing states. Give a short definition for them.

Melting:

_____

_____

Freezing:

_____

_____

Boiling:

_____

_____

Question 3

Freddie has written a report about the water cycle, but he wants you to help him finish it! Fill in the gaps that he has left, to give him a hand.

'Evaporation' is the process of liquid water turning into gas form, which is called _____.
This happens when the sun provides enough heat to a body of water.

The water vapour rises into the air, until the air becomes too _____ for the vapour to remain as a gas. This is called condensation. The water vapour – a gas, turns into water droplets – a _____. Eventually, enough droplets combine to form full clouds.

In a full cloud, the water droplets are too heavy to be held up by the air. So, they begin to fall to Earth in the form of rain, sleet or snow. This is called _____.

This precipitation will fall into lakes and rivers, which will eventually carry it back into the _____. Or, it will fall onto the ground – being absorbed by the earth – from which plants will get the moisture they need.

However, the process doesn't really have an end or beginning – it is a cycle, which means all of the steps we have just discussed are always happening all at the same time!

ANSWERS TO STATES OF MATTER

Question 1

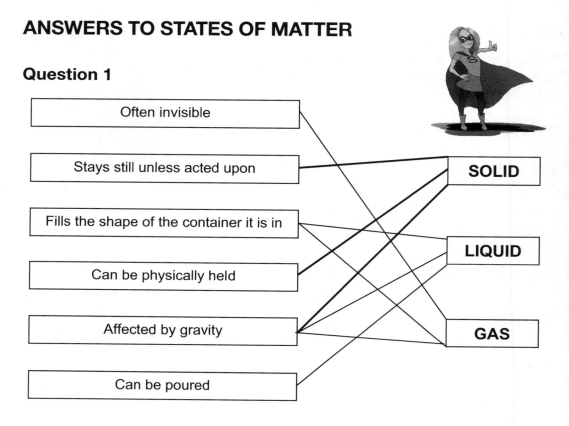

Often invisible	SOLID
Stays still unless acted upon	LIQUID
Fills the shape of the container it is in	GAS
Can be physically held	
Affected by gravity	
Can be poured	

Question 2

Melting: 'Melting' is the process that solids go through to become liquids. This occurs when a solid is heated enough to reach its 'melting point' – the temperature where it can no longer remain as a solid and becomes a liquid.

Freezing: 'Freezing' is the process that liquids go through to become solids. This occurs when a liquid is cooled enough to reach its 'freezing point' (for water this is 0°C). The freezing point is the temperature at which a liquid will become a solid.

Boiling: 'Boiling' is the process that a liquid goes through to become a gas. This occurs when a liquid is heated enough to reach its 'boiling point' (for water this is 100°C). The boiling point is the temperature at which a liquid will become a gas.

Question 3

'Evaporation' is the process of liquid water turning into gas form, which is called <u>water vapour.</u> This happens when the sun provides enough heat to a body of water.

The water vapour rises into the air, until the air becomes too <u>cold</u> for the vapour to remain as a gas. This is called condensation. The water vapour – a gas, turns into water droplets – a <u>liquid</u>. Eventually, enough droplets combine to form full clouds.

In a full cloud, the water droplets are too heavy to be held up by the air. So, they begin to fall to Earth in the form of rain, sleet or snow. This is called <u>precipitation</u>.

This precipitation will fall into lakes and rivers, which will eventually carry it back into the <u>sea</u>. Or, it will fall onto the ground – being absorbed by the earth – from which plants will get the moisture they need.

However, the process doesn't really have an end or beginning – it is a cycle, which means all of the steps we have just discussed are always happening all at the same time!

THE
REVISION
SERIES

PROPERTIES
OF MATERIALS

PROPERTIES OF MATERIALS

Different materials (objects and liquids) have different properties. This means that they have different characteristics, like hardness or conductivity. Different properties make certain objects more suited to different jobs.

The 'properties' of a material can also tell us how it will behave in certain situations, like being exposed to heat or electricity.

There are also things we can do that will change a material's properties, some of which are reversible, and some of which are not.

Our superhero Scarlett is going to teach you the properties of materials, in FIVE main sections!

1. **Physical properties**

2. **Solutions and mixtures**

3. **Reversible changes**

4. **Irreversible changes**

5. **Separating mixtures**

So, let's get started with physical properties!

PROPERTIES OF MATERIALS

Physical properties

HARDNESS

Some materials, like steel, are extremely hard. This is a measure of how much force something can take before it changes shape. These materials are also very hard to scratch, which makes them useful for cutting or drilling into materials that are softer than they are.

Although seemingly similar, the hardness of a material is different to its strength, which is a measure of how much something can be stretched before breaking.

TRANSPARENCY

Some materials, like glass, are **transparent** (see-through). This makes them useful for windows – which provide shelter while letting natural light pass through them.

Some materials are **translucent**. This means that they are partly see-through – they let light pass through them but it is often difficult to see clearly through them. For example – green and brown glass bottles are translucent.

Some materials are **opaque**. This means that they are not see-through – they do not let any light pass through them. For example – the blinds on your windows, and most everyday objects, are opaque.

PROPERTIES OF MATERIALS

CONDUCTIVITY

If a material is a good **conductor**, it is good at letting things like heat and electricity pass through it. Some materials are good conductors of heat, some are good conductors of electricity, and many can do both.

For example, most metals are good thermal and electrical conductors.

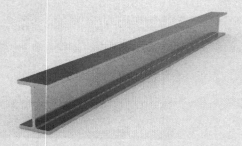

Materials that are good conductors are very useful for humans:

- Metal saucepans allow heat from a hob to pass to food.
- Copper wires allow electricity to pass from the mains to appliances like your television.
- Radiators are good conductors of heat. They are very good at emitting heat – they can spread it around a room.

Materials that are poor conductors are called **insulators** – they hold onto heat and electricity well, and do not pass it to other things.

Things like oven gloves are made from fabrics that are good insulators, so they don't transfer heat from a boiling pan to your hands!

Other common insulators are wood and plastics.

MAGNETISM

Some materials, for example (most) metals, can be moved by magnets. Humans use magnets for many things. For example, compasses use magnetic fields to show us north, south, east and west.

Special cranes use high-powered magnets to sort magnetic material from non-magnetic material.

PROPERTIES OF MATERIALS

Solutions & mixtures

Some materials and substances can be mixed with water to create a **solution**.

A solution is a **liquid** that contains more than one material or substance. For example, a cup of instant coffee is a solution of water and coffee granules, which may contain milk and sugar.

Solids that break down to form a liquid solution are called **soluble** materials. The process a solid goes through to become part of a solution is called **dissolving**.

(**Insoluble** materials include things like sand, rocks, wood and metal.)

Soluble sugar and insoluble sand

Often, substances that dissolve in water look like they have disappeared completely. For example, if you add salt to water, it will eventually be dissolved by the water, forming a transparent solution.

However, the salt has not disappeared; it has simply been mixed together with the water. This breaks down the salt and makes it lose its colour, but the same amount of salt is in the water before and after it has dissolved!

PROPERTIES OF MATERIALS

It is possible to get the original solid substance back from a solution after it has dissolved. For example, it is possible to extract salt in its solid form, from a liquid saltwater solution. This is done by boiling the solution; this causes the water to turn into gas form (steam/water vapour), leaving the salt in solid form.

So, the change that salt goes through by becoming part of a solution is a **reversible** change.

Let's look at reversible changes, as well as irreversible changes, in more detail:

Reversible changes

A **reversible change** is a change of state (e.g. solid to liquid), brought about by a change in the environment surrounding an object (such as heat/cold), **which can be undone** without anything being lost in the process.

<u>For example:</u>

Imagine taking an ice-lolly out of the freezer and putting it in a cup on a table. Leave it for around ten minutes until it melts, leaving a liquid and the stick.

➤ **The lolly has changed state** – from solid to liquid.

The lolly is now in liquid form, having lost all the properties and characteristics of a solid that it once had.

But, it can be changed back! Put the cup and stick into the freezer, and wait around four hours. The liquid will have refrozen, turning the lolly back into a solid.

➤ **The lolly has changed back to its original state** – from liquid to solid.

Although the lolly will have a different shape – it will now be the shape of the inside of the cup – its mass (how much ice lolly there actually was) will not have changed.

PROPERTIES OF MATERIALS

Irreversible
changes

An irreversible change still refers to a change in state brought about by an outside force (like heat or cold), but one that cannot be undone. **An irreversible change is a permanent change.**

For example:

Imagine throwing a stick of wood onto a fire. The heat of the fire breaks the wood down into a dust-like substance (ash) – this process produces smoke, a gas.

➢   **The wood has changed state** – to dust and smoke.

Now, no matter what you do, it is impossible to change the ash and smoke back into wood.

➢   **The ash and smoke cannot turn back into wood.**

Separating mixtures

Many mixtures (of both solid and liquid materials) can be separated out into their individual components. Different mixtures require different techniques to separate them out. Separating mixtures is very useful to humans, so let's look at a few common ways to do this.

SIEVING

Sieves are made from a wire mesh that is held in a bowl-shape by a frame, or is just a flat piece of material. The mesh allows solids of a certain size to pass through it, while keeping larger particles on the other side.

- Sieves are used to separate solid particles of different sizes.

FILTERING

A filter works similarly to a sieve, but resembles something closer to a sheet of paper rather than a bowl with holes in.

Filter paper has extremely small holes, which means it can be used to separate solids from liquids as it allows a liquid to pass through it while keeping the solid on the other side.

- Filters are used to separate insoluble solids from liquids.

EVAPORATING

Evaporation can also be used to separate solids from liquids. If something solid has dissolved in a liquid, it is sometimes possible to separate this mixture by boiling away the liquid, which will leave the solid in its original state (before it dissolved).

- Evaporating separates soluble solids from liquids.

Question 1

Preston and Blaze are discussing the hardness of materials.

Preston says:

"If a material is hard, it is difficult to dent or put a hole in."

Blaze says:

"No, if a material is hard, then it is good at putting holes in other stuff!"

Who is right? Preston, Blaze, or both of them? Explain your answer:

_____

_____

_____

_____

_____

_____

Question 2

Anil has just built a new superhero sanctum for the team.

Look at the picture and write down what the materials are made out of, their properties, and how they are best suited to their uses.

Window:

Copper wire:

Granite work surfaces:

Brick wall:

Slate roof:

Fridge door:

Question 3

1. In general terms, what makes something change state? (E.g. solid to liquid or liquid to gas.)

   _____

   _____

2. Describe how melting chocolate is a reversible change.

   _____

   _____

   _____

   _____

3. Describe how scrambling eggs is an irreversible change.

   _____

   _____

   _____

   _____

4. Is dissolving sugar in hot water a reversible or irreversible change? Give reasons for your answer.

   _____

   _____

   _____

   _____

Question 4

In the box are some common changes of state. Help Lalita by sorting them into the columns underneath, titled 'Reversible change' and 'Irreversible change'.

Boiling water

Burning paper

Cooking meat

Melting candle wax

Freezing water

Mixing cement and sand to make concrete

REVERSIBLE CHANGES	IRREVERSIBLE CHANGES

Question 5

Below is a list of mixtures. In the boxes provided under each one, write down **sieve, filter** or **evaporation** to show which method you think would be best to separate that particular mixture.

1. Sand and gravel

2. Salt and water

3. Rice and water

4. Coffee granules and water

ANSWERS TO PROPERTIES OF MATERIALS

Question 1

Both Preston and Blaze are right. A harder material will not be dented or penetrated by any material softer than it, and it will also be able to put a hole in anything softer than it. Therefore, due to the fact that a 'hard material' will be harder than most materials, it is possible to say that it is difficult to dent a hard material, and that hard materials are good at putting holes in other things.

Question 2

Window: The window is made of glass. This is suited to its use, as it prevents rain and cold from coming into the sanctum, but allows plenty of natural light to enter.

Electrical wire: The electrical wire is made from copper, which is a great conductor of electricity, allowing the sanctum to receive power. Copper can also be worked down to a useful wire shape, and is fairly light. Finally, copper does not waste much energy through heat – maximising efficiency.

Work surfaces: The work surfaces are made from a hard and strong material such as granite – this makes it durable, which is helpful for everyday use. Granite can also be easily cleaned, and is very resistant to heat.

Wall: The wall is made from bricks, which are very strong and resistant to rain and wind.

Roof: The roof is made from slate rock, which is also resistant to weather, and able to be shaped into useful flat tiles.

Fridge door: The fridge door contains magnets, which ensure that it does not accidentally open and allow heat inside. Magnets will hold the door closed, but not so strongly that it is impossible to open.

Question 3

1. An outside force makes something change state – most commonly a change of temperature. This can either be an increase in temperature (heating), or a decrease in temperature (cooling).

2. Melting chocolate is a reversible change, because it is possible to turn liquid chocolate back to its solid form. This is done by putting it in the fridge, in order for the liquid to cool. The shape of the chocolate will have changed, but the amount will not have changed.

3. Scrambling eggs involves exposing raw eggs to high temperatures. This permanently changes them in a way that is not reversible. Exposing scrambled eggs to low temperatures, for example, will not make them raw again.

4. Dissolving sugar in hot water is a reversible change, as it is possible to get the sugar back into solid form after it has been dissolved (broken down) by the water. This is done by evaporating away the water, by boiling it. Once all the water in the pan has turned to gas, the solid sugar will be the last thing remaining.

Question 4

REVERSIBLE CHANGES	IRREVERSIBLE CHANGES
Boiling water	Cooking meat
Freezing water	Mixing cement and sand to make concrete
Melting candle wax	Burning paper

Question 5

1. Sieve
2. Evaporation
3. Sieve
4. Filter

Chemistry Mock Paper

Questions

30 minutes

First Name	
Middle Name/s	
Last Name	
School	
Date of Birth	D D / M M / Y Y Y Y

1 In the box are some examples of permeable and non-permeable rocks. Sort them into the table given below, into the columns titled 'Permeable rocks' and 'Impermeable rocks'.

> **Sandstone**
>
> **Granite**
>
> **Slate**
>
> **Marble**
>
> **Chalk**

PERMEABLE ROCKS	IMPERMEABLE ROCKS

5 marks

2 Explain why hard rocks have always been useful to humans.

_____

_____

_____

2 marks

3 Soil has 4 main ingredients. Out of the six things listed below, two are incorrect. Put ticks (✔) in the boxes next to the correct ingredients, and crosses (✘) in the boxes next to the incorrect ingredients.

Water	

Sugar	

Rock	

Dead plants and animals	

Air	

Wood	

4 Explain why soil is vital to all living things on Earth.

_____

_____

_____

5 Dave the triceratops is going to tell you what he knows about fossils. In the space given below, write down whether you agree with him or not, and the reasons for your response.

Fossils take millions of years to form, and millions more to be found! So, any animal found as a fossil today no longer exists. I've been dead for 65 million years! ☺

3 marks

6 What is the final fossilised skeleton made out of? Circle **one**.

Rock   **Minerals**   **Sediment**   **Bone**

1 mark

Match the descriptions of the properties of solids, liquids and gases to the correct options by writing **1**, **2** or **3** in the boxes given.

SOLID	☐
LIQUID	☐
GAS	☐

1. This state of matter has a pretty loose shape, so it can flow downhill and be poured out of a container. Humans have got pretty good at holding it, but this cannot be done with bare hands!

2. This state of matter has a loose shape, so is hard to hold in one place. It will also spread itself out to fill the space it finds itself in.

3. This state of matter will generally stay the same shape unless someone or something does something to it. Humans can hold it in their hands and control its movement.

☐

3 marks

8 Describe the changing states shown by the pictures.

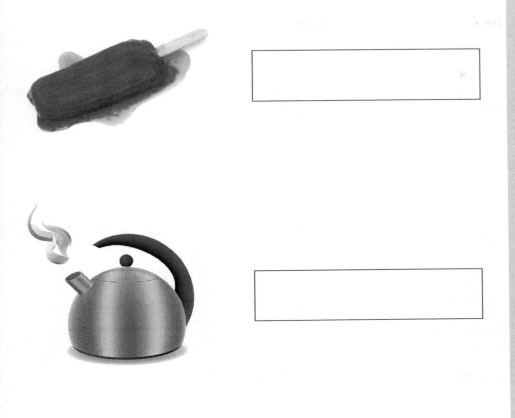

3 marks

9 Label the following diagram, which shows the three main stages of the water cycle.

[_____]

[_____]   [_____]

3 marks

10 Jordan says: "**The water cycle has a clear beginning and a clear end.**"

Do you agree? Give a reason for your response.

_____

_____

_____

2 marks

11 Kettles are usually made of metal. They are able to boil water with a heating element located at their base.

Metal is a good choice of material to make kettles from. Why? Put a tick (✔) in the box next to the correct reason.

It is opaque	☐
It is shiny	☐
It is heavy	☐
It is a good conductor	☐

 12 Copper is a good choice of metal to make electrical wires from, because it is a good conductor of electricity. What other properties does copper have that makes it a good choice? Give two properties.

_____

_____

_____

13 Katie has bought a packet of corn kernels from a supermarket. She puts the packet into her microwave and cooks them on a high heat for 4 minutes. During the 4 minutes, she could hear several popping sounds.

She takes the packet out of the microwave and pours its contents into a bowl. The kernels are now warm, and have turned much lighter in colour. They have also become larger, and appear to be fluffy. A new material has been produced.

a) What has Katie made?

_____

b) Is the change that the kernels have gone through reversible?

_____

c) How do you know this?

_____

_____

3 marks

14 Gemma and Jacob have made a mixture of seawater, sand, and pebbles.

a) What should they use to separate the pebbles from the rest of the mixture? Circle **one**.

     Sieve   **Filter Paper**   **Evaporation**

b) What should they use to separate the sand from the rest of the mixture? Circle **one**.

     Sieve   **Filter Paper**   **Evaporation**

c) If they wanted to get the salt from the seawater in solid form, what could they do?

_____

_____

_____

_____

_____

4 marks

END OF TEST

ANSWERS

1.

PERMEABLE ROCKS	IMPERMEABLE ROCKS
Sandstone	Granite
Chalk	Slate
	Marble

2.

Answers should mention how hard rocks are used for tools, early humans made weapons for hunting out of hard rocks, and how buildings made of hard rock give us shelter.

3.

The boxes next to water, rock, dead plants and animals, and air should be ticked.

The boxes next to sugar and wood should have a cross in them.

4.

Answers should mention that animals rely on plants for food, which need soil to grow. So, animals (including humans) could not survive without soil

5.

Answers should mention that Dave is correct. The process of fossilisation takes millions of years, and fossils take millions more years to be found. So, fossils are remains of long extinct animals. Dave should not be happy that he's dead, though.

6.

Minerals should be circled.

7.

Soild should have number 3 next to it.

Liquid should have number 2 next to it.

Gas should have number 1 next to it.

8.

The box next to the ice cream should say **melting**.

The box next to the kettle should say **boiling**.

The box next to the ice tray should say **freezing**.

9.

The box pointing to the clouds should say **condensation**.

The box pointing to the raindrops should say **precipitation**.

The box pointing to the water vapour rising should say **evaporation**.

10.

Jordan is incorrect. Answers should mention how the water cycle is an ongoing process that never stops or starts.

11.

The box next to 'It is a good conductor' should be ticked.

12.

Answers should mention that copper can be easily worked down into a wire shape, and is an efficient carrier of electric energy – little is wasted through heat.

13.

a. Katie has made popcorn.

b. The change is irreversible.

c. Answers should mention that because a new material has been created through cooking, it is impossible to make this disappear, un-cooking the kernels.

14.

a. **Sieve** should be circled.

b. **Filter paper** should be circled.

c. Answers should mention that they could boil the water off, turning it into gas form. This would leave salt them with salt in its solid form.

WANT MORE SCIENCE PRACTICE QUESTIONS?

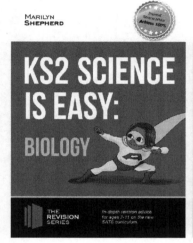

How2Become has created two other FANTASTIC guides to help you and your child prepare for their Key Stage Two (KS2) Science SATs.

These exciting guides are filled with fun and interesting facts for your child to engage with, to ensure that their revision is fun, and their learning is improved!

Invest in your child's future today!

FOR MORE INFORMATION ON OUR KEY STAGE 2 (KS2) GUIDES, PLEASE CHECK OUT THE FOLLOWING:

WWW.HOW2BECOME.COM

NEED MORE HELP WITH OTHER SCHOOL SUBJECTS?

Get Access To
FREE
Psychometric Tests

www.PsychometricTestsOnline.co.uk